STONEHOUSE
TO
PAINSWICK
IN OLD PHOTOGRAPHS

'GOODBYE PAINSWICK', SEPT. '90. A party leaving Castle Hale in September 1890. This photograph has plenty of interest. The classic country house scene, with gardener and stable-lad holding the horses while bonnet bedecked ladies make ready for the off. Note the gentleman in his mortar board.

STONEHOUSE
TO
PAINSWICK
IN OLD PHOTOGRAPHS

COLLECTED BY
ALAN SUTTON

ALAN SUTTON
1989

Alan Sutton Publishing
Gloucester

First published 1989

British Library Cataloguing in Publication Data

Stonehouse to Painswick in old photographs.
1. Gloucestershire, history
I. Sutton, Alan
942.4'1

ISBN 0-86299-401-2

Typesetting and origination by
Alan Sutton Publishing
Printed in Great Britain by
Dotesios Printers Limited

CONTENTS

INTRODUCTION

Stonehouse is not a town that is usually identified along with Painswick. Stonehouse is in the vale and predominantly brick whereas Painswick is in the Cotswolds and virtually all stone. Yet the two towns are less than five miles apart as the proverbial crow flies.

In the series of books on Gloucestershire in Old Photographs, Stroud has been amply provided for in the volumes by Stanley Gardiner and Lionel Padin. In this book I am therefore trying to do justice to the area to the north and west of Stroud, while omitting any reference to Stroud itself.

The photographs have not been catalogued in chronological sequence nor subject matter sequence. Instead, I have followed a journey cycle beginning at Selsley. We start on the Common and then progress down the winding lane to Middleyard and King's Stanley. There is a slight digression to Ryeford and then we are back on course to Leonard Stanley and Frocester. From Frocester on to Eastington, and then on to a major section of the book covering the town of Stonehouse.

Leaving Stonehouse we meander around narrow and ancient roads from Standish to Haresfield and Harescombe. We touch upon Brookthorpe and then leave the vale and travel up the western escarpment of the Cotswolds to Edge. We then move to another major section, that of the town of Painswick. The journey sequence follows on to Pitchcombe, Whiteshill, Ruscombe and Randwick and finishes with Cainscross and Ebley.

Basically the book takes in the two valleys of the Frome and the Painswick Stream, with the Cotswolds and the Vale of Gloucester as if in a radial arc from the pivotal point of Cainscross.

The photographs come mainly from postcards and reflect the heyday of the genre – the two decades from 1900 to 1920. Other postcards are included right up to the 1950s, but it is the Edwardian and First World War periods that provid the mass of material reproduced in this book.

One of the pleasures in producing this book has been in reading the messages on the backs of some of the postcards. Many postcards were pristine or virgin cards that have never suffered the test of the General Post Office. Others are well travelled cards containing a variety of missives and messages from the days before the common use of the telephone. Many carry simplistic, almost naive messages reflecting the age of elementary education. A good example of this is the card shown in this book of the Old Crown, King's Stanley; the message being: 'Dear Flo, I am having a lovely time down here. I don't want to come back, but I shall be home on Tuesday. With love, Ivy.'

The destination address was in Swindon and this, along with many similar cards, shows that the Stroud area was a popular holiday resort! One other holidaymaker was a brash Londoner who posted the attractive Leonard Stanley postcard on 26 July 1905, at the same time complaining of the inadequacy of our Gloucestershire postcard range (p.29): 'Have had a glorious time at Nailsworth & am now staying in Stroud or rather just out of it! The postcards are very dreadful here, tho' the scenery is so lovely. Love to you all, E.S.'

At least E.S. had the decency to acknowledge the scenery, although it would have been interesting to know of the quality of postcard he was used to. Moving forward 15 years, we have a more cultured, middle-class holidaymaker in Edge (p.102): '24 May 1919. One attraction on my tours is the picturesque churches in the villages. They look so charming and inviting, and the atmosphere in the interiors seems so different – more reverent, than our city churches. This is Edge church nr. Painswick, small but s'nice. Avec amour, Leon x.'

One cannot help but wonder, with the innocent and almost juvenile style of this message, if the writer was not a young but surviving veteran of the First World War. May is a beautiful time on the Cotswolds, especially on the escarpments, with their beech trees and their translucent fresh greenery. This may well have struck a chord with Leon and put him in his poetic mood. Presumably the recipient of this innocence was his young beloved, stuck in the grime of some large city. Unfortunately, Leon does not give a destination address and the card was presumably sent in an envelope.

One other recurring theme in postcard messages is that of ill health. With a much better over-all standard of living and diet, and with modern medicine – especially antibiotics – we take our health for granted. In Edwardian times, and even much later, this was certainly not the case. Many postcards reflect this state of being and show messages from sick folk reporting their current state of health to relatives and friends or, alternatively, from convalescents, writing home from their recuperative haunt in the Cotswolds. This next card is the latter, postmarked 15 December 1939 and also from Edge. It is a Christmas card back to friends in Aberdeen (p.101). 'Hillside, The Edge. A very happy Xmas to you all. How do you like my new home? I am very happy here & gradually gaining strength, everyone is so kind and friendly. The country is beautiful, can see the R. Severn from my window. Love ...' (name illegible).

THOMAS MOSS, of Andrews Cottage, Brookthorpe in 1895.

It is very difficult, when looking at old photographs, to get a feel of what life was like in this area at the beginning of the century. Certainly many of the places are recognizable and many individuals in the photographs can be identified by readers as parents or grandparents in more youthful form; but what was life like? How different was life without television or, more fundamentally, electricity? In more rural areas there was not even gas and the motor car was quite a rarity. There were no supermarkets and sugar and flour came loose and not pre-packed. There was no possibility of buying out-of-season vegetables and fruit flown from Israel, and one certainly did not eat pork in the summer! But, apart from these banalities, what were folk like without these trappings of late twentieth-century luxury? Part of the answer may be gleaned from the writings of visitors like Joseph Arthur Gibbs, John Moore, C. Henry Warren or our local author Laurie Lee. To give a flavour prior to our first photographic excursion, I quote at some length from C. Henry Warren in *A Cotswold Year*:

HILL FARM, EDGE, 1895.

'At any time, and whatever they are doing, countrymen move slowly and with deliberation; but never quite so slowly as now. It is the time for retrospection. Old Jesse Gable came over to help mend my wall this morning, and as he stood expertly weighing the stones in his hand, he talked to me about the Woodend of years ago; for he was born here. He talked to me about the changes he had seen in the farm, told me about the people who lived here when he was a boy, and about Jake and Abel, two old brothers who lived in a house the ruin of which I can just see peeping through the trees, until Jake hanged himself for misery and Abel died soon after. He told me about an old woman who used to live in this cottage many years ago. "Her ol' man," he said, "was a terror. Used to frighten her out of her skin. Watched her like a cat watchin' a mouse. If she went up to the village, she runned there an' she runned back agen – so's she could have a couple o' minutes' gossip with her cronies." Jesse pulled out a misfit stone and searched for a better one. When he found one to his liking, he continued: "But when her ol' man died she couldn't say good enough about him to anybody: used to sing her George's praises night an' day. Yes, an' every mealtime she continued to lay his place at the table, till she died . . . Still, she was a pleasant body, and a rare one for her garden."'

Like our convalescent, C. Henry Warren lived at Edge and from his tale of Woodenders from the turn of the century, and the holiday-makers, or con- valescents, or middle-class romantics we move on to the pictorial record which they – by courtesy of the postcard photographers and publishers – have left for us and for posterity. A record which, for the photographers and publishers, was a commercial exploitation of a market need and, for us, is an invaluable glimpse of our locality before and after the war to end all wars.

Finally, I must say a word about the postcard photographers whose work is reproduced in this book. Not all of the pictures reproduced here are postcards, but the majority most certainly are. Some were real photograph postcards, some were collotype postcards. Collotype is a continuous-tone printing process, and until the last few years the Cotswold Collotype Company still carried on this trade, first in Wotton-under-Edge, and subsequently in Nailsworth. The Cotswold Collotype was formed out of the Cotswold Publishing Company (cPc), and many of the images in this book came from their output. Their most prolific period was from about 1909 to 1915, and you will see my approximate dating for their pictures mainly falls within this range.

Another local photographer and card publisher who should be mentioned is Mark Merrett. Born in 1862, he moved to this area from Bermondsey c. 1888. First of all he was in partnership with his brother George, but this was dissolved in 1895. He later was in business with his brother Rayner, and they traded under the name of Merrett Brothers for many years. The charming picture on page 1; a picnic scene, is from the output of Merrett Brothers. The photograph was probably taken by Mark Merrett's wife, as it shows all of her family – except herself! Mark semi-retired in 1924, but continued photography from his studio in Belle Vue Road, Stroud until shortly before his death in 1945.

The other postcard publishers are too numerous to mention, but without their work our ability to glimpse into the past would be a much more difficult job.

Alan Sutton
Hydefield
Uley

ACKNOWLEDGEMENTS

This book has only been made possible by the help and generosity of Mr Fred Rowbotham and Mr Wilfred Merrett. Both have dug deep into their photographic collections to provide a large portion of the contents of this book.

In addition I thank Mr Donald Emes, Mr Stanley Gardiner, Mr Michael Handford, Gloucestershire Record Office and the Gloucester City Library for their assistance in this volume.

Uncaptioned preliminary pages illustrations:

Page 1. A PICNIC PARTY, probably in the Haresfield area c. 1906. From left to right: Martha Gay (junior), Lizzie Durden, –unknown–, Annie Gay, Maria Budding, John Gay and Martha Gay (senior).

Page 4. A detail from the picture on page 133.

Page 5. THE EASTINGTON SCHOOL BRASS WHISTLE BAND, c. 1907. The boy in the front row, second from left, was Tommy Howell; killed in action during the First World War.

Page 7. THE ORIGINAL CAINSCROSS AND EBLEY CO-OPERATIVE SOCIETY SHOP, c. 1902.

EASTINGTON SCHOOL MORRIS DANCERS, at the May Queen celebrations in 1921.

SECTION ONE

Selsley, King's Stanley and Leonard Stanley

THE NEW INN, SELSLEY. Two views taken some years apart. The top picture is older and shows the outside wooden skittle alley in a derelict state. The bottom picture shows the alley after repair, c. 1920. The signs above the door show the licensees as being Leonard Hogg for the top picture, and Burnal Hogg in the bottom. Note the unmade roads with fine Cotswold stone chippings.

SELSLEY.

A THATCHED COTTAGE IN SELSLEY c. 1900. The woman behind the cottage appears to be in traditional costume although she is rather indistinct. The road here is also shown before it was given its macadamized surface. The surfaces in these districts were invariably Cotswold stone dust and chippings. It sets as hard as concrete in dry weather, but gives off a fine dust. In wet weather it is a sticky yellow and makes marvellous footprints on the best of carpets.

The cottage has now disappeared, replaced by two post-war bungalows.

Selsey Village

SELSLEY VILLAGE C. 1912. This view was on a card postmarked 1912, although it could have been taken a few years earlier. It shows the same thatched cottage as on page 15 and a preponderance of flag poles. I wonder why they are such a feature of Selsley at this time?

Note the quantity of elm trees in this picture, they were a strong feature of the Severn vale and were incorporated in many hedgerows.

TWO VIEWS OF SELSLEY. The top picture was taken just down from the junction leading up to Selsley Common and the road to Uley and Dursley. The trees in this picture have either gone or been replaced – in fact, there are more trees now than then, but otherwise most of the buildings are still standing, with more buildings now infilled. The bottom Edwardian picture is taken on the western boundary of Selsley adjoining Middleyard.

A BONFIRE ON SELSLEY HILL. In celebration of King George V's coronation, June 1911. Sir William Marling is the elderly gentleman in dark suit and bowler hat, fifth from left.

THE WEAVERS ARMS INN, MIDDLEYARD. There is no date on this card, although the costume and ladies' hairstyles suggest the late Edwardian period. Possibly c. 1910.

KING'S STANLEY BAPTIST CHAPEL, Middleyard. The card was postmarked 1911, although the picture could be some years earlier. This card was one of the Cotswold Publishing Company's Gloucestershire series.

HIGH STREET, KING'S STANLEY, c. 1912. A comparison with the view today is interesting. Although the basic street scene is little changed, a vast number of building alterations have occurred over the last 80 years. One very minor point is that Tudor Houses now have the plaster removed from the front as well as the end gable. Note the absence of intrusive telephone and electricity wires.

TWO DEFUNCT KING'S STANLEY PUBLIC HOUSES. The date of the Star is difficult to determine. Note the cheerful old lady at the gate, no doubt checking up on the photographer! The card for the Old Crown was postmarked 1920.

ANOTHER DEFUNCT PUBLIC HOUSE, The New Inn, postmarked 1936.

THE GREEN, KING'S STANLEY, C. 1905.

CASTLE STREET, KING'S STANLEY, showing village pump and railings, postmarked 1912.

INSIDE VIEW OF STANLEY MILL, difficult to date, but possibly as early as 1900. The picture is very faded and barely reproducable, but included in this collection because of its interest.

TWO VIEWS OF RYEFORD STATION. The Midland Railway station on the branch line which, one mile further to the east, forked out to termini at Stroud and Nailsworth. The close-up of the station house is postmarked 1914.

J. Price & Sons, Ltd.,

Have at their Ryeford Nursery
one of the finest collections of

Exotic Flowering Plants

..in the county.

Large supplies of Choice Flowers for their rapidly extending
Bouquet and Wreath Trade are always ready for cutting.

Floral Designs of all kinds arranged by Gold and Silver
Medallist, made from freshly cut
Flowers, sent carefully packed to any part of the country and
guaranteed to arrive in good condition.

**Floral Designs artistically arranged from 3/6 to 5 guineas
and upwards, satisfaction guaranteed.**

J. P. & Sons have had the honour of taking the Highest Awards for Bouquets
and Wreaths at some of the principal Flower Shows in the country, in competition with the leading exhibitors of Floral Designs, and also the honour of
supplying Bouquets for presentation to

**Members of the Royal Family and to many Operatic
and Theatrical Notabilities.**

J. PRICE & SONS, Ltd., Nurserymen, Seedsmen
. . . and Florists,

Telephone: 145x STROUD.   **Ryeford and Kingstanley Nurseries,**
IYI, STONEHOUSE.   **and London Road, STROUD.**

RYEFORD NURSERIES from a 1903 advertisement.

HAYWARDSFIELD INN, Ryeford, c. 1907.

BRINGING IN THE HARVEST. This marvellous picture is labelled 'harvesting nr. King's Stanley'. The picture shows orchards on the slopes of Pen Hill, with Stanley Woods to the right-hand side. The photograph is difficult to date but is probably c. 1920. It is interesting, when studying photographs for captioning, to see if any clues exist for dating or for throwing light on the purpose behind taking the photograph in the first place. Many photographs were taken for picture postcards and many to note special events. This picture was probably taken specifically for a postcard and it is evident that it has been posed. The stooks of wheat were probably random but the photographer has found a good position between them, set the house nicely in centre with a balanced back-drop of hills and woods, and then asked the farmer with the cart to oblige him. Leading the horse is the farmer, the late Harry King. What else can one add, apart from to say that it is most likely August and, by the length and position of the shadows it is early evening.

LEONARD STANLEY, a view of c. 1915. At one time Leonard Stanley was a thriving market town with two annual fairs; one on St Leonard's Day, 6 November and another on St Swithin's Day, 15 July. A disastrous fire in May 1686 reduced much of the town to rubble and it never subsequently recovered its previous stature.

LEONARD STANLEY, two views of Church Street, both c. 1905. The bottom view is the card carrying that scurrilous message about local postcards referred to in the introduction.

SEVEN WATERS, LEONARD STANLEY, 1905. This scenic view is taken looking west towards Frocester, before the days of parked cars taking up all of one side of the road.

COTSWOLD STORES LTD, a later picture of the same shop shown opposite. This photograph c. 1924.

THE OLD BATH ROAD, c. 1905, pictured before it received a tarmacadam surface.

CHURCH ROAD AND THE CHURCH, LEONARD STANLEY. The top picture dates to c. 1912 and shows some of the Priory Farm buildings on the right-hand side. The bottom view is considerably later, possibly c. 1930. Grove Cottage is shown before the growth of virginia creeper. The thatched buildings on the right have all been replaced by more functional but much less attractive farm buildings.

THE CORONATION BONFIRE at the Knoll, June 1911. This was another bonfire to celebrate the coronation of King George V.

PRIORY FARM, 1928, showing the remains of the old priory in the farm buildings.

LEONARD STANLEY from the church tower c. 1908.

Frocester and Eastington

FROCESTER POST OFFICE. These two views were taken only a few years apart. The top ramshackle view is postmarked 1905 and shows thatch in the last stages of decay. The bottom picture shows the new tiled roof although, in many other respects, the picture is similar, especially showing the nonchalant way in which the middle ground-floor shutter is carefully stowed away during hours of daylight!

FROCESTER POST OFFICE. Either Frocester had a superabundance of postal facilities or the function changed to new premises. Which ever was true, this postcard view was taken c. 1912.

THE GEORGE AT FROCESTER, 1905. For some reason these premises now have a sign outside reading 'Royal Gloucestershire Hussar'. What a daft name. It was built as The George and after carrying that name for over two hundred years it seems irreverent to change it. To most people in the Severn Vale it is still known affectionately as the 'Frocester George'. A Georgian building, it was purpose-built as a coaching inn for the busy turnpike road from Gloucester to Bath.

Frocester Hill.

TWO VIEWS OF FROCESTER HILL. The old turnpike road up Frocester Hill ran to the north-east of the road shown here. It was extremely steep, necessitating an additional pair of horses for every coach, supplied from The George. In 1782 a new turnpike road, with easier gradients, was opened through Nailsworth and this new road took much of the traffic from Gloucester to Bath. To compete with the new road, this new cut was made in 1784, thereby avoiding the steep hill and the necessity of passing through Nympsfield.

SEVERN VIEW FROM FROCESTER HILL.

TWO VIEWS OF THE ENTRANCE ARCH TO FROCESTER COURT. The bottom picture is postmarked 1908 and the top view, looking down the drive to the village of Frocester, is probably slightly later.

FROCESTER ROAD, EASTINGTON, in 1918. This picture epitomizes what we have lost since 1976. The majestic elms in nearly every hedgerow and roadside boundary. Apparently (so my book of trees tells me) the English Elm is thought to have been introduced to the Vale of Berkeley from the south of France as a selected local form of Field Elm and spread out from there! Fancy that – the home of the English Elm – which now, happily, is fast growing again, hopefully to be spared the ravages of those nasty little beetles.

THE CROSS, EASTINGTON. The top picture, looking towards Claypits, is c. 1900. The bottom picture, looking towards Stonehouse with the blacksmith's shop on the left and Columbia Place in the centre, is postmarked 1904.

COLUMBIA PLACE, Eastington, postmarked 1918.

THE KING'S HEAD HOTEL, Eastington, c. 1920.

TWO MORE PATRIOTIC PUBLIC HOUSES. These pictures of the Britannia and the Victoria are both c. 1920, but they are difficult to date precisely and could be ten years either way.

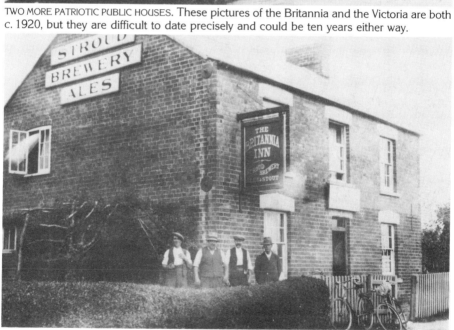

MIDDLE STREET, EASTINGTON. Here we run into serious problems with dating. The costume would seem to indicate to me a date for both pictures of between 1903–1909 but the bottom view is postmarked 1931. This cannot be accurate. The local stores must have been using ancient stock for the message on the card from a holidaymaker reads 'We have been to Framilode today on the sands, this is a little place near here'.

MEADOW MILL, EASTINGTON, c. 1912.

INSIDE BOND'S MILL, EASTINGTON, c. 1915.

EASTINGTON WESLEYAN CHAPEL, c. 1910.

WHEATENHURST UNION WORKHOUSE, postmarked 1907. This building probably dates back to 1838. Most union workhouses in the country were erected in 1838 or 1839 or, alternatively, adapted from existing buildings following the Poor Law Reform Act of 1837.

NEW BRIDGE, EASTINGTON, over the river Frome, postmarked 1918.

CHIPPENHAM PLATT COAL WHARF at Eastington Bridge, c. 1890. Captain and Mrs Stephen Chandler on *Nellie*, owned by white-bearded Mr Zacharia Whiting, the village coal merchant, standing on the wharf.

EASTINGTON BRIDGE, C. 1910, with a Severn trow on the left and a two-donkey-towed long boat coming under the bridge. The boatmen referred to the donkeys and horses as 'the animals'. The cottages on the right have been demolished although the lock house still stands.

EASTINGTON BRIDGE, C. 1928. This bridge was built in 1924 to replace the original eighteenth-century bridge and facilitate road widening. This new bridge was subsequently swept away after the building of the M5 in the early 1970s.

EASTINGTON BRIDGE. This postcard is not dated but the schoolboy's garb, together with that of the lady on the roadside opposite, would seem to indicate the 1940s. As the road sign is back in place, this must be late 1940s. The tarmac and curb on the left look fresh and the right-hand balustrade of the bridge appears different to that in the previous picture. Was this possibly the result of a road- and bridge-widening exercise?

PIKE LOCK, EASTINGTON, c. 1910. John White, lock-keeper is on the right. He was subsequently drowned in Pike Lock.

EASTINGTON BRIDGE AND PIKE LOCK, 1973. This photograph was taken only a few months before the bridge was demolished. Sadly, the new bridge replacing this fine structure has very limited headroom and is yet one further impediment to the reopening of the canal.

THE NEW INN, Newtown, with three intrepid travellers c. 1920.

ROVING BRIDGE, NEWTOWN. The top picture shows the Stroudwater Canal when it was still in commercial use. This photograph was taken c. 1905 and is postmarked 1907. The bottom photograph, taken in 1973, shows the dereliction of years. The last commercial toll on the canal was paid in 1941 and the canal was formally abandoned, by Act of Parliament, in 1954.

THE CO-OP VAN c. 1910. The Cainscross and Ebley Co-operative Society was extremely successful in the late nineteenth and first half of the twentieth centuries, with many branches in the area. In the 1960s it was incorporated with its Gloucester equivalent to become the Gloucester & Severnside Co-operative Society Limited. This particular van driver is often in local photographs. For some reason he appears in many photographs with his horse and van. Is that the same man on page 96? The exact location of this picture is unknown. It could be as far away as Dursley or Cam but is probably around the Stonehouse/Frocester area.

Stonehouse

OCEAN RAILWAY BRIDGE, 1949, with a train heading south on the main Gloucester to Bristol line, just at that time being nationalized from LMS to British Railways.

THE OCEAN, STONEHOUSE. Possibly the smallest ocean in the world! The turning area on the Stroudwater Canal, with the LMS railway bridge centre distance.

Stonehouse.   *St. Cyril's Church.*

THE STROUDWATER CANAL AND ST CYR'S CHURCH. The card is postmarked 1904.

WYCLIFFE COLLEGE SCOUTS on the Stroudwater Canal.

WYCLIFFE COLLEGE BOATHOUSE with bathers in the Lower Field c. 1925.

STONEHOUSE COURT, the morning of 30 May 1908, with the ruins still smouldering from the fire the night before.

STONEHOUSE COURT. The Court was built in 1601 in the traditional flattering form of a letter 'E' for Elizabeth. It was restored in 1906 by Sir Edwin Lutyens but much of his work went up in flames. However, although the damage was severe, and the fire gutted the inside, sufficient was left for the building to be rebuilt.

HOFFMAN'S BALL-BEARING FACTORY, 1941, a photograph retrieved from Luftwaffe archives after the war. Ball-bearings were an essential part of most engines and machines. Obviously this factory was identified as a strategic target.

THE HOME GUARD, a photograph of 1941 or 1942 showing the Stonehouse Brigade.

THE SPA INN, Oldend, c. 1926.

THE BAKER FAMILY at the Spa Inn in 1902, celebrating the coronation of King Edward VII. Mr Baker was the licensee at that time.

GLOUCESTER ROAD, looking towards Stonehouse with Gordon Terrace on the left-hand side. In the immediate left foreground is the turning to Woodcock Lane. Photograph, c. 1930.

GLOUCESTER ROAD, looking towards Stonehouse with Miss French's School at Hillview House on the right-hand side. The Royal Oak is in the distance on the left before the GWR bridge. Photograph, c. 1920.

GLOUCESTER ROAD, looking towards Gloucester with the Royal Oak on the right. Note the unsurfaced road at this time. The card was postmarked 1906.

HARRY PEGLER, in Stonehouse on his way back towards Stroud after picking up wooden cases of 'England's Glory' matches from Gloucester. Photograph, c. 1900.

THE COUNCIL SCHOOL, looking back towards the village, c. 1909. Where the trees are shown is now the row of shops in Elm Road.

THE COUNCIL SCHOOL, the chalked board reads '1920 Stonehouse Schools 1'.

Stonehouse.   Upper High Street.

HIGH STREET, c. 1910. A picture taken from just past the GWR bridge looking back into the village. The card was postmarked 1915 but the photograph was probably taken a few years earlier.

PARK HOUSE, HIGH STREET. Decorated for Queen Victoria's Diamond Jubilee in 1897. The monkey puzzle tree in the garden is the same tree shown in the picture above.

THE GREEN, c. 1927, showing the village pump and the War Memorial, looking across towards the Globe.

THE GREEN, 1887. A photograph from virtually the same viewpoint, just outside Park House, looking across the green to the Globe. The decorations were for Queen Victoria's Golden Jubilee celebrations. Note how scruffy the green was at this time, some 40 years before the top picture was taken. The pole in the middle of the green was the maypole.

QUEEN VICTORIA'S DIAMOND JUBILEE CELEBRATIONS on the green in 1897. This photograph was taken from outside the Globe looking back across the green. Note the lady on a tricycle in the foreground.

THE MAYPOLE ON THE GREEN, C. 1910, with the conservatory of Park House behind.

ORCHARD HOUSE, High Street, 1912; with the children of the house, Wilfrid, Stella and Raymond Hudson, on the right.

THE CROWN AND ANCHOR HOTEL. The top picture shows the original Commercial Inn, c. 1890. The central portion of the building was demolished and replaced as shown below. This is the building that survives today. The bottom photograph is c. 1912. The card it was on was postmarked 1915.

Stonehouse.   *The Crown and Anchor Hotel.*

HIGH STREET, OUTSIDE THE CROWN AND ANCHOR. The top picture, c. 1925, shows an open top double-deck bus. The bottom picture is slightly later, c. 1930, showing Hughes the chemist, on the right, and the Co-operative stores in the centre.

HIGH STREET IN 1897. Two photographs taken during Queen Victoria's Diamond Jubilee celebrations. These were probably part of a larger collection taken of Stonehouse during the celebration week. The top picture is looking towards Gloucester. Park House is visible centre distance. The bottom picture shows the recently rebuilt Crown and Anchor on the left. The gentleman talking to the shopkeeper is the Revd Farren White, vicar of St Cyr's.

CAINSCROSS AND EBLEY CO-OPERATIVE SOCIETY, Stonehouse branch, in 1914.

HIGH STREET, C. 1948, with the Co-operative Society in the centre. The two shops on the right are A.J. Gillow, butcher; and Harrison, baker.

HIGH STREET, looking towards Stroud and the junction of Regent Street on the right. The top picture, c. 1927, with Timbrell's the newsagents on the left. The bottom picture, c. 1947, shows the new post office built in 1933, on the left.

HIGH STREET, looking towards Gloucester. The top picture c. 1910, the bottom picture, with the Woolpack sign on the left and post office on the right, c. 1957.

A GAS EXPLOSION. The location of this photograph is unknown, the description given was Stonehouse but I cannot locate a similar building. Perhaps it was all demolished and rebuilt. The suggestion of a gas explosion is purely a guess. By the costume, the date must be c. 1880 but any further information would be very welcome.

THE CONGREGATIONAL CHURCH, c. 1910. The church was demolished in 1964. The site is now covered by the National Westminster Bank.

LOWER HIGH STREET, c. 1904, looking in the direction of Gloucester, with the cedar tree outside the Congregational Church visible on the left-hand side.

BATH ROAD, C. 1900. The junction of Regent Street is on the immediate right.

WYCLIFFE COLLEGE, the first school group in 1883.

WYCLIFFE COLLEGE METHODIST CHURCH. The tower was built as a memorial to Old Boys killed in the First World War.

FIRE AT THE METHODIST CHURCH. Wycliffe College Methodist Church was gutted by fire in November 1939. The tower survived but the chapel itself was virtually destroyed.

OLD COTTAGES AT HAYWARD'S END. These rather ramshackle but picturesque cottages have long been demolished.

A GWR AUTOCAR AT STONEHOUSE STATION, c. 1915. These pioneering trains, with the engine embodied in the carriage, ran regular services between Chalford, Stroud and Stonehouse.

A LOCAL TRAIN on the 'up' line of what had been the GWR station before nationalisation. This photograph taken in 1964.

THE MIDLAND RAILWAY BRIDGE, photographed on 8 April 1973, just six days before demolition commenced.

THE MIDLAND RAILWAY STATION. The top picture c. 1920, the bottom picture rather later, probably c. 1938.

CORONATION BONFIRE, on Doverow Hill, June 1911. Yet another of the sequence of bonfires built to celebrate the coronation of King George V.

THE LEAGUE OF NATIONS PIONEERS, Stonehouse Branch, c. 1922. The League of Nations was created out of the ashes of the First World War. The League was subscribed to by the signatories of the Treaty of Versailles on 28 June 1919 and formally came into being in January 1920. It was the precursor of the United Nations and this photograph shows local enthusiasm for the ideals it embodied, after the carnage of the war.

STONEHOUSE TOWN PRIZE BAND, C. 1905.

STONEHOUSE FLOWER SHOW pushball competition, 2 August 1906.

A COSTUME FOOTBALL MATCH at the recreation ground, Stonehouse, 1904.

MRS PENN'S CONCERT PARTY PANTOMIME, c. 1920, held in the church hall in the Laburnum.

MISS BRIGHT'S BIBLE CLASS, held in St Cyril's Road, off Queen's Road, c. 1915. The GWR station can be seen behind.

ST CYR'S SCOUT GROUP. Back row, from left to right: Fred Rowbotham, Revd J.B. Gale, Stanley Fawkes. Middle row: Stan Joyner, Lionel Smith, Ginger Brown. Front row: Tom Edwards, Stanley Penn, Nat Russel, Melvin Townsend, Basil Arnold.

ST CYR'S CHOIR, 1947.

STONEHOUSE AFC, 1908–9 season.

STONEHOUSE AFC, a photograph taken 25 August 1949 – just three days after I was born. Part of the interest in compiling a book such as this is the unexpected information it throws up. When studying this picture, I recognized a familiar face – my first cousin – Terry Phillips, in the centre, dark-haired with folded arms. Although Dursley born and bred, he played two seasons at Stonehouse.

THE BRUSHWORKS FC, 1928, after beating Walsall 5–1. At the rear, Mr A. Meluish. Third row, left to right: E. Fry, J. Lawrence, A. Scobell. Second row: Mr. A. Gravel, G. Short, S. Miles, G. Horle, C. Elmer, J. Elmer, A. Trigg. Front row: F. Aston, J. Bailey.

UPPER MILLS, a letter-heading engraving c. 1890.

THE BRUSHWORKS STAFF, c. 1955.

THE REGAL CINEMA. The first Regal was converted from the old church hall in the Laburnum in 1933. It was burnt down in a fire in September 1936. The new Regal, below, was built in 1939. After serving for many years as a panel beating shop it has recently been demolished. Both of these photographs were taken from poor quality originals.

THE STONEHOUSE BRICKWORKS. Now the site of the Rosedale estate.

Standish, Haresfield, Harescombe, Brookthorpe and Edge

ST. NICHOLAS, Standish, probably photographed by the Revd Andrew Freeman at some time around the First World War. The surface on the original photograph, together with the material the print was produced on, first led me to believe that this was a very early photograph. I have often seen photographs from the 1860s and 1870s produced on similar material, and with the same surface effect. It may well be a very old print, alternatively, it may be c. 1915, and photographed and developed by the Revd Freeman himself if he was an amateur photographer.

STANDISH COURT, or more to the point, the ruins of the gatehouse in 1925.

STANDISH HOUSE, c. 1920. The house was built in 1830 and, in the early-twentieth century, became Standish House Hospital, presumably as a convalescent hospital for some of the wounded from the trenches.

CHILDREN PLAYING at Standish Hospital c. 1920.

STANDISH HOSPITAL, two views, both probably 1920s. The top picture shows part of Standish
House behind.

Men's Wing,
Standish House Stonehouse.

Holy Well, Haresfield.

HOLY WELL, HARESFIELD, C. 1898. The picture is rather posed, with the little girl being too shy to look up. Inside the well a boy is winding up a bucket of water.

HARESFIELD STATION. Those were the days, pre-Beeching, pre-1963, when you could travel to Gloucester on the stopping train, calling at each halt; Coaley Junction, Frocester, Stonehouse, Haresfield, and then pull in at Eastgate Station, Gloucester. The irony is that there is now a real demand to return to these stopping trains but, in the rush to cut the system down in size, many of the facilities that would now prove useful were destroyed. The British disease of under-investment and chronic shortsightedness.

This photograph is probably c. 1905 and, at the time, the railway company would have been the Midland Railway; not becoming part of the London, Midland and Scottish until the railway groupings of 1922.

THE HARESFIELD BEACON & RAILWAY HOTEL. Built in 1855 to the design of Francis Niblett, an ecclesiastical architect responsible for many nineteenth-century church restorations in Gloucestershire. The Co-op bread van is in the upper picture. See page 52.

HARESFIELD POST OFFICE. Fortunately we have some legend on the back of this card that sets the scene: 'Dear Geo., This is when Liz & me went to Brookthorpe & got a puncture in Haresfield & that young man standing there mended it for us, & just as he finished mending it and we were coming away someone took our photos. My bike is over the other side of the station. J.' An Edwardian stamp is on the card so this is *c*. 1905.

CROMWELL HOUSE, HARESFIELD HILL.

HARESFIELD VILLAGE, 1908.

HARESFIELD RECTORY, postmarked 1921, although the actual photograph was probably taken some years earlier.

HARESCOMBE. A winter scene, presumably on a very still day by the look of the water. The date of this picture is difficult to assess. It could have been as early as 1880 or as late as 1920. I searched in vain on the copy of this photograph looking for dating clues – all to no avail and then, when I checked back, the original card had a postmark! 1907.

BROOKTHORPE, with the Four Mile House on the right-hand side, 1933.

BROOKTHORPE COURT AND CHURCH, c. 1910. The Court was built in the sixteenth and seventeenth centuries, and restored in the nineteenth century. St Swithin's Church is mainly thirteenth century.

STOCK END, THE EDGE, C. 1950. The country writer, C. Henry Warren lived at Edge in the 1930s. The following paragraph is his description of the view from his window. 'Away in the distance, some twenty-five miles away, are the Malvern Hills, like a crouching lion. Over to the left is May Hill, even farther away, but so clear today that I can see its golden crest of bracken shining in the sun. Behind these, in dim blue outline, rise the Sugar-loaf Mountain and the Welsh hills; and between them and me lies the rich plain of the River Severn, that twists like a silver serpent through the trees and is finally lost behind Robin's Wood Hill, where the red roofs of Gloucester gash the green landscape with factory chimneys and gasometers, aerodromes and slums.'

HILLSIDE, THE EDGE.

ST JOHN THE BAPTIST, EDGE, C. 1920. The church is relatively modern, having been built in 1865. This is the church that our poetic Leon referred to in his message, mentioned in the introduction.

GLOUCESTER HOUSE, now known as the Edgemoor. This picture, c. 1925, before the many additions to the building.

SECTION FIVE

Painswick

PAINSWICK BEACON, two views, c. 1909. The bottom picture is looking towards Robinswood Hill, with Gloucester beyond.

TOCKNELL'S COURT, c. 1920. The main house was built c. 1665, the pillars surmounted by stone lions in the garden wall were added by a later owner in 1716.

CASTLE GODWYN, this fine house, nestling in the valley, was built c. 1730. This photograph is c. 1905, the card was postmarked 1910.

A LANE NEAR THE BEACON, C. 1910. This picture typifies the difference between unmade tracks then and now. Then, the tracks had three ruts!

PARADISE, April 1927. The Adam & Eve can be seen in the top left-hand corner.

THE ADAM & EVE INN. Both pictures c. 1920. The licensee at this time had the cheerful name of Thomas Tombs.

PARKWALL. This photograph by W. Ridler probably dates back to 1880 judging by costume.

A VIEW OF PAINSWICK, c. 1915, taken from just below Bull's Cross.

BROOKHOUSE MILL alias the Pin Mill, c. 1900.

FORMER PIN MILL STORE in King's Mill Lane, 1895. Demolished after the First World War.

NEWTOWN, c. 1920. Newtown is not as recent as it sounds. New Street and 'Novo Vico', or 'New Town', is first referred to in a deed dated 1400.

STAMAGES LANE, c. 1908. This photograph is taken looking towards Painswick. The building in the foreground, presumably the mill, has long been gone. The cottage behind is still there, though much altered and extended. The field on the right-hand side is now grown over with trees.

STAMAGES LANE. A very old photograph, possibly dating back to the 1880s. This photograph gives the opposite view to that on page 111. The mill building can be seen more clearly. The cottage behind is still there but now looks far more regal, having had major reworkings, re-roofing and an extension.

KING'S MILL, c. 1899. Waterfall at the head of the mill pond.

THE COURT HOUSE. Two views, both from the very early part of this century. They are difficult to date but the top view is probably the older of the two, c. 1905, the bottom picture c. 1920.

The Verlands

(Late the Old Vicarage),

Painswick,

Gloucestershire.

Under the personal management
of the Proprietors—

Mr. & Mrs. Russell.

Premises now being enlarged, Seven more Bedrooms
being added in consequence of great demand.

Superior Board

Residence.

Per Week, or Special
for long periods.

Tariff on Application.

THE VERLANDS is beautifully situated on the Cotswold Hills at Painswick; is high and bracing; commanding lovely views of the surrounding country; pronounced by visitors to nearly equal anything of the sort in England; has charming Lawns and Gardens; shady walks; Tennis and Croquet.

Golf Links quite near.

Close to Church and Post Office.
Bath Room (hot and cold).

Sanitation and Water perfect.
Every Home Comfort.

Post and Telegraph Office : Painswick.
Station : Stroud (Midland and G.W.R.) 3½ miles.

THE VERLANDS, 1903. The house at the Verlands or 'Far Lands', as its original uncorrupted form would have been, was built in 1828 as the vicarage. By 1903 it had been transformed into this hotel.

VICARAGE STREET, C. 1905. One of my favourite photographs in this book. Mrs Tilly Wright
with the pram, Mrs Annie Walkley holding the child and Tom Gyde centre background.

One of the joys of compiling an old photograph book is the great help given by local
residents of the older generation. I was standing in Vicarage Street, holding a clip board,
checking the photograph against existing buildings and making notes when an elderly
resident called out to me, 'Fine dry day ain't it' – and, almost in the same breath without
waiting for me to reply – 'What you about then?' I briefly explained my task and he almost
grabbed the photograph and quickly reeled off the names of those in the picture as if it had
been taken only yesterday. We were then joined by a contemporary of his who corroborated
the evidence. I was told about the White Horse further up the street, the site of which now
forms a new road junction. A delightful ten minutes was spent in boyhood memories of
Painswick from the time of the Great War – and then it was time to be off on my further
peregrinations.

VICARAGE STREET, c. 1895. This picture is taken from almost the identical position as that on page 116. The shed roof on the left is not in such a precarious state and the shrubbery has not yet grown. Spot the other differences.

THE PAINSWICK FIRE BRIGADE, c. 1890.

DOVER HOUSE, c. 1900. This fine house was built c. 1720, a splendid example of early Georgian domestic architecture. The pillars and finials remain in place but, unfortunately, the gate and side railings have gone – given way to the inevitable need for vehicular access.

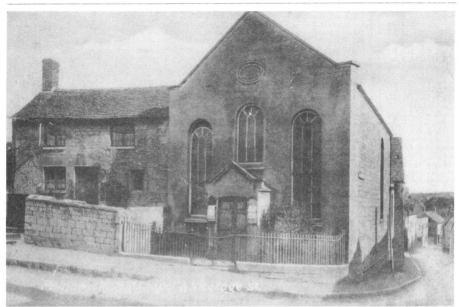

PAINSWICK PRIMITIVE METHODIST CHAPEL, Vicarage Street, c. 1905. Now an estate agent's office!

ST MARY'S HOUSE NURSING HOME as it then was c. 1920.

TWO VIEWS OF BISLEY STREET, showing the Red Lion centre background. The top picture from *c.* 1900, the bottom photograph slightly later, possibly into the 1930s.

BISLEY STREET, c. 1895. The enlargement of the children has not worked too well, mainly because the source of this view was a small collotype plate and not an original photograph. This is where I get rather confused because the pub on the left is called the White Horse. Was the original White Horse here and, after this pub was closed, was the licence and name transferred to Vicarage Street?

BISLEY STREET looking up towards Gloucester Street, c. 1908.

FRIDAY STREET, with the Bell on the right-hand side. The Bell was demolished by a bomb on 14 June 1941. Several bombs landed on the town, presumably jettisoned by a lone German raider who was searching for the G.A.C. factories at Hucclecote and Brockworth. Altogether three people were killed in this raid and several were injured. Several houses in the town were demolished. The photograph above is c. 1915.

FRIDAY STREET. Spot the difference. These two pictures must have been taken within days or a few weeks of each other. The car would seem to indicate mid-1920s. My assumption of closeness is based upon the notices in the window. What similarities or differences can you spot?

The Gables, Painswick.

FRIDAY STREET looking towards Bisley Street, with the building that was the Bell on the left-hand side. Presumably this ceased to be a pub shortly before this, c. 1930.

THE CROSS, looking towards Bisley Street and Vicarage Street, c. 1898.

TWO VIEWS OF TIBBIWELL, looking towards the Cross. The top picture is the older, c. 1910. The bottom photograph – with tarmacadamed roads – c. 1920, possibly even later.

TWO VIEWS OF TIBBIWELL, looking towards Bull's Cross. These are of a similar age to the facing pair of pictures; the top picture possibly, c. 1915, the bottom one, c. 1920, or slightly later.

Painswick Church. East Gate.

PAINSWICK CHURCH EAST GATE, C. 1905. The bottom view is considerably later, probably 1930s, but both pictures show the iron pillars and gates which have since gone.

THE STOCKS, c. 1910. Somehow these pictures make the stocks look larger than they really are.

A HOUSE NEAR THE CHURCH, photographed and drawn in 1902 by Horace Field and Michael Bunney for publication in their book *English Domestic Architecture of the XVII and XVIII Centuries*.

A·HOVSE·NEAR·THE·CHVRCH·PAINSWICK·GLOSTERSHIRE·

PAINSWICK CHURCH after being struck by lightning on 10 June 1883.

A VIEW FROM THE TOWER, showing recently planted trees in the churchyard and the Temperance Hotel at the top of Victoria Street, 1902.

VICTORIA STREET c. 1920. The Temperance Hotel has now become the Cotswold Private Hotel.

PAINSWICK CHURCH, c. 1930. The railings, gates and pillar finials shown here have all now gone.

THE PAINSWICK YEWS. The trunks are now thicker, the sign has been replaced and the railings have gone. Otherwise there is little change since this picture was taken c. 1915.

NEW STREET, c. 1910.

THE MUCKRAKERS, c. 1900. This was, presumably, a common occurrence with dirt roads. A gathering of working men, probably paid on the parish rates, to rake over the roads. Was this some sort of annual festival? Not all of the men look like road men and some are obviously in family groups. Note the foreman on the left, with note-pad in hand. Also, the army corporal on leave joining in the fun.

THE PAINSWICK POSTMEN, c. 1905. All standing outside the post office in New Street (shown on page 137). The postman, second from left, looks a jolly soul.

TWO VIEWS OF NEW STREET. The top picture shows the old post office c. 1915. The arched gateway on the left was enlarged to make a vehicular access as illustrated in the next card, postmarked 1938. By the arched doorway is a display of picture postcards. The proprietor of the shop was E.T. Spring, also the publisher of this card.

THE FALCON HOTEL, C. 1904. Note the girl on the left by the railings and the boy in the centre, both with hoops and sticks. The exposure time for this photograph must have been several seconds; a boy walking up the street is blurred as is the horse's head, bobbing up and down.

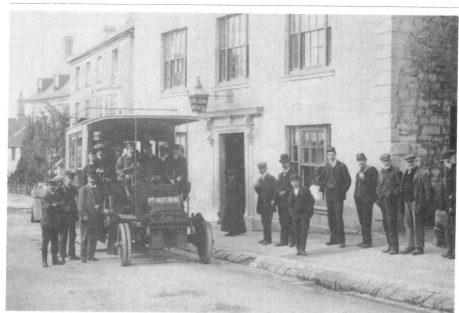

THE FALCON HOTEL, with a motor bus outside. Judging by the growth of the shrubs and creeper two doors down, this is probably also 1904. Perhaps earlier in the summer to the picture on the facing page.

THE FALCON GARAGE, c. 1928.

THE TOP OF BISLEY STREET, *c.* 1895. This picture, together with those on page 121 and the top of page 143, are all from small collotype prints and have been hand-labelled on the back 'July 1922'. This cannot be right. I believe they are from around 1895. They could be slightly later and it is unlikely that they are much earlier. Notice the shop window in the photograph above and compare that with the window shown in the top picture opposite. The evidence is overwhelmingly against a 1922 date. The street sign, the dirt road and the costume of the little girl convince me that this is mid-to-late 1890s.

THE STAR INN, at the crossroads of New Street, Bisley Street and Gloucester Street c. 1908. Notice that compared with the picture on page 140, when London House has been substantially altered. Notice, in particular, the new coping and the disguised chimney in the coping.

CHELTENHAM ROAD, a Cotswold Publishing Company postcard view, c. 1915.

TWO VIEWS OF GLOUCESTER STREET. The top picture c. 1905, the bottom picture c. 1930.

GLOUCESTER STREET, c. 1895. There are subtle differences between this picture and the top picture opposite. The house in the centre does not appear to have been a shop at this time and still retains a wooden gate. The picture opposite shows the fence in a more rickety state, gate gone, the shrubs cut back and hollyhocks growing in abundance.

THE ALEXANDRA HOME 1908. The Home was a sanatorium for tuberculosis sufferers. This postcard is quite rare, being one of the first published under the CPC (Cotswold Publishing Company) imprint. The company was bought from the Frith family in 1907 and the equipment was moved to Wotton-under-Edge in 1909. This card reads 'CPC Charfield' on the back. It must, therefore, be between 1907 and 1909.

THE GYDE ORPHANAGE, C. 1915. The orphanage was built only a year or so before this picture was taken. It looks as if some landscaping is going on at the time of this photograph.

PAINSWICK HOUSE. The date of the photograph is unknown and difficult to assess, but probably 1920s. The house was built in the 1730s and its original name was Buenos Aires.

Pitchcombe, Whiteshill, Ruscombe, Randwick, Cainscross and Ebley

PITCHCOMBE, two views c. 1922.

PITCHCOMBE, a village view, *c.* 1925. According to A.H. Smith, in the English Place-Name Society volumes on *The Place-Names of Gloucestershire*, Pitchcombe probably takes its name from 'Pincen's Cumbe', 'Pincen' being a woman's name and 'Cumbe' being a valley. One early recorded rendering of the name was 'Pychencumbe' in the year 1211.

PITCHCOMBE HOUSE in the 1920s. The house was built for Thomas Palling c. 1740.

THE EAGLE INN, PITCHCOMBE, c. 1915. The Eagle was on the A46 on the right-hand side of the road towards Painswick. The licensee at this time, according to the sign on the building, was Sarah Ann Young.

THE EAGLE INN. This picture was taken in 1895, probably by Florence Henrietta Maitland of Brookthorpe. This is part of a series, and others can be seen on pages 103 (detail of page 110), 110 and 150. Also the pictures in the introduction, pages 6 (detail of page 150) 9 and 10.

WRAGG CASTLE FARM, Pitchcombe in 1895. This delightful picture shows a relaxed family group of woman and children. Note in particular the small child in traditional bonnet. A detail from this picture is reproduced in enlarged format on page 6.

WHITESHILL FROM THE CHURCH TOWER, c. 1918.

KITES NEST FARMHOUSE, Whiteshill, c. 1925.

MAIN ROAD WHITESHILL, looking up towards the Woodcutter's Arms, c. 1920. The road was considerably narrower at this time.

RUSCOMBE in 1956. This relatively modern picture of Ruscombe shows the Congregational Chapel towards the right-hand side. The picture was taken looking north, with Ruscombe Wood on the left.

TWO VIEWS OF RUSCOMBE. The top picture, c. 1900, looking north-west towards Ruscombe Wood. The bottom picture, looking south-east towards Whiteshill and Stroud. The Congregational Chapel on the left was built in 1825.

MOOR HALL, RANDWICK, c. 1904. Moor Hall was built in the late-sixteenth century and the date 1582 is over one of the doorways. The hall was restored c. 1920 and this picture was taken nearly 20 years before restoration.

THE VINE TREE INN, RANDWICK, c. 1902.

RANDWICK. This charming picture of children was postmarked February 1911 and so was photographed in 1910 or before. The building on the right is the Rising Sun Inn.

TWO VIEWS OF RANDWICK. The top picture is the earlier, probably c. 1905. The bottom picture is c. 1930 and photographed from the church tower.

RANDWICK 18   VIEW FROM CHURCH TOWER

AUTO-CAR NO. 50 AT EBLEY CROSSING, c. 1910. Number 50 was built in 1907 and designed to seat 70 passengers. The engine was built into the coach body.

WALTER MERRETT and his wife Rosa c. 1920. Walter retired from an umbrella business in Bow, London, and carried on his trade in a modest way from Mark Merrett's shop in Ebley. Notice the picture postcards on the left-hand side. See the note about Mark Merrett on page 11.

CAINSCROSS looking towards Stroud, c. 1929.

CAINSCROSS, looking towards Dudbridge, c. 1929. This photograph was taken on the same day as that opposite. Judging by the shadows, it is late afternoon and the children opposite are on their way home from school. Can you tell which picture was taken first?

EBLEY MILL, C. 1908, in its less expensive form.